EARN MONEY WITH YOUR INSTAGRAM ACCOUNT FOR 2019

GET THOUSANDS OF REAL FOLLOWERS QUICKLY,
EARN MONEY WITH EACH PHOTO YOU UPLOAD WITH
YOUR PERSONAL ACCOUNT

Gaston Echevarria

Table of Contents

Introduction The reality of the market

Every month, more than a billion people connect to Instagram, interact with the content and publish it on the platform.

Far from being one of the most visited and often used social media platforms, even more so than Facebook, Instagram has become the "primary" platform for serious business owners, advertisers and marketers looking to build their business online.

And even though Instagram is 100% free to start - and you can have a new Instagram account up and running in less than five minutes.

The truth of the matter is that the vast majority of business owners, advertisers and sellers are not using Instagram in the right way to build their business or create the kind of financial future they have always dreamed of.

Honestly, most of the Instagram market is little more than "traditional marketing" applied to the digital world - and that's no longer going to cut the mustard.

No, if you are going to make your Instagram marketing leave the park and really turn it into a powerful channel for marketing, you have to know exactly what you are doing.

On top of that, because you're facing an established and stiff competition, you also need to take advantage of as many shortcut checklists as possible to get to the top as quickly as possible.

Here are some critical tips and tricks in this quick checklist that will help you do exactly that.

Let's dive right in!

What strategy should I follow?

Most people run their marketing directly off the rails at first, not even realizing that all their Instagram marketing and was built on a sand base and not concrete.

Most people simply throw different marketing approaches at the Instagram wall and expect something to stick, rather than taking a real systematic and focused approach to create a marketing that really has a chance to work.

> ➢ *But you won't!*

You won't, since you're reading this quick checklist and following all the tips and tricks we could share, you're going to have an almost unfair advantage over the competition to create a truly effective marketing that really works.

You will be able to start from the beginning (where you need to create that solid base) and build from there.

➢ *Identify your perfect potential customer*

The first thing you have to do (even before creating a new Instagram account) is to create a clear and crystalline image of who your perfect potential customer is.

You need to know what they're most interested in getting from you, what they're most interested in seeing and interacting with Instagram, and the "hot buttons" that force them to move from

Launching your marketing campaign six months (or better yet, a year) in advance with a plan for each of the content you are going to publish on a very specific day and as part of a very specific marketing campaign gives you an almost unfair advantage over the rest of your competition.

By establishing an understanding that you will have to create content for a three times a week launch, you are not only able to create those messages in advance and prepare them for prime time, but you are also able to find the right piece of content to publish at a given time to fit in with all the other marketing approaches you are using.

With a content marketing calendar, you may be working on a Valentine's Day campaign, for example, in mid-June, with content to be published on Instagram that goes hand in hand with the Valentine's Day campaign you have been running from late January to mid-February next year.

On top of that, you can actually start automating your Instagram marketing when you take this type of approach.

Because you have all your content created and ready to use, you can then create script programs or outsource the actual publishing work to someone else, freeing up your time so you can concentrate on other high-performance business activities without having to worry about how you're going to prepare an advertising approach that day.

This is a game that changes things, and you have to be 100% sure that you're doing it.

ALL in your power to systematize,
automate and delegate most of your work.

You must grow up as fast as possible.

Growth, growth, growth - Grow as big and as fast as you can

The next stage after laying the foundation and marketing of Instagram focuses entirely on growing its follow-up as fast as humanly possible.

Instagram does a lot of the heavy lifting for you, helping to recommend your Instagram account to others automatically and even actively promoting your account through Instagram Day Postings, hashtags, etc., but you really want to take possession of your Instagram marketing from the beginning to make your account grow as big as you can as fast as possible.

After all, the world's largest content, perfectly tailored to your ideal customers, will be worth NOTHING unless you are receiving the eyes and active participation of the people who have chosen to follow your Instagram account.

Without trackers, all your efforts are completely wasted - so you have to build that track from the ground with lightning speed.

Here are some quick tips to help you do exactly that!

> ***Instagram Influencers***

Instagram's influencers - the most frequently tracked, engaged and active

accounts in your market or industry -
have the ability to raise any account they
interact with regularly, as well as any
account that interacts regularly with them.

You have to do everything in your power
to get the attention of these Instagram
influencers in your industry or market so
that they start actively promoting the
content you provide (and we'll show you a
way to do it in just a second) OR you have
to try to "steal their thunder" as much as
possible by mentioning them in your own
content so that your followers start paying
attention to you as well.

Instagram's marketing is fast becoming
a kind of arms race, with large accounts
posting new jobs per hour instead of a
daily or even weekly update.

Big accounts - we're talking about

accounts with hundreds of thousands or even millions of followers - need a lot of activity to keep up with their hungry followers, and that means they need a huge amount of original content that they have the opportunity to share.

That's where you, as the "smallest operator," comes in.

Because you don't have to feed the same kind of beast (yet), you can afford not only to create content for your own Instagram account, but also content for the main influencers of the Instagram account.

By creating content that you give to these influential people to share with their 100% free followers (though with attributions and tags that return to your account), you can do them a favor while serving their own needs.

This type of accounts are very happy to enter into this type of agreements.

They receive a lot of free, high-quality content that they don't have to work hard to create, keep their fans happy, and associate with newcomers from the same industry.

You'll also benefit from the additional exposure you get from these Instagram influence accounts - and before you know it you'll have floods of followers diving headlong into your account, making you an influencer too!

The contests in instagram

Another great approach to growing your account quickly is to hold regular contests where you actually give away high quality items or services in your Instagram account in exchange for more followers.

This is a proven, true and surprisingly effective marketing tactic and technique that has been in use long before Instagram was thought of.

All you have to do is fulfill your part of the bargain - actually, give away any product or service you've promised - and they cost you a little up front, but when you actively monetize your Instagram account, you'll realize that the return on investment is well worth it.

The bigger the item, the more exciting the service and the more valuable the gift, the more action you'll get and the more followers you'll accumulate.

If you are in the golf niche, for example, giving away a sleeve of balls is just going to move the needle. However, giving a trip to Pebble Beach will make you swim in more followers than you know what to do with them.

Of course, that trip to Pebble Beach is going to cost a lot more than a sleeve of balls, but as mentioned earlier the return on investment is going to be worth it.

Instead of picking up a handful of followers for $12, you could pick up 10,000 new followers or more for $2000.

The commitment should be obvious.

> ➢ *Create multiple monetization channels with Instagram*

At the end of the day, new followers are not cash in the bank unless you really start monetizing your followers and your Instagram account.

The easiest way to monetize your Instagram account is to simply use your Instagram account and Instagram content as an entry level to your marketing funnel.

You'll be able to push visitors and followers deeper and deeper into your marketing materials, turning at least some of them into paying customers - and that has a fairly reasonable return on investment.

Of course, there are other ways to monetize your Instagram account - and even if you decide to sell your own products and services, you'll want to follow some of these avenues to maximize your influence on social media and create multiple sources of income.

To begin with, you can look for other companies in your sector - competitors or those offering complementary services - and offer to provide them with "sponsored content".

Basically, you become an affiliate of your company and any sales you make through your Instagram account will pay you a commission.

This is how many of the "Instagram models" make their money online, posting photos of themselves and training equipment or using training supplements provided by other companies and getting a share of the affiliate sales they drive.

These people are making a steady income from this type of affiliate marketing on their own, so it is definitely worth investigating.

There are many ways to monetize Instagram, and hopefully, this quick checklist has shed a little more light on the subject for you to move forward.

Adaptation

From now on, I will directly explain you the topics you need to maximize your Instagram account. Let's get started!

If you are interested in maximizing profits and turnover, then customizing your product is a great way to do it. There are several reasons why this is vital to your business. Here are five reasons why you should;

1. Attention to detail pays off
-

Here, the focus is on ways that will make your product stand out from the crowd. Not only do they stand out for a classy logo and brand, but they also show that you are taking care of your product.

This will push you to design everything about your product down to the last detail that customers will be able to see and make them want to buy.

2. *Understand your customers and their trends*

When you begin to adapt your product, it means that you are understanding the needs and desires of your customers. If you conduct research on what your customers want and match it to your product line, then your message becomes very powerful. Producing products according to customers' needs and preferences will not only save you money, it will also help your customers realize how much they care and how socially responsible you are.

3. *Customization helps a product*

stand out

Adapting your products has many advantages and helps you distinguish your products and differentiate yourself from the competition. If your products seem to have taken some time to be planned before reaching the market, then it is likely that what you offer will keep a strong foothold in the market by keeping your business going for years to come.

4. *Preventing counterfeiting*

To effectively sell your product, let customers feel it and come to a conclusion for themselves rather than exposing it to them. Instead of reciting a long list of benefits and features, custom tailoring shows your service or product in action, making your product interesting for a second look.

Comprehensive packaging services

By adapting your products, you also have the advantage of getting numerous offers from other related service providers. For example, you can sign a managed inventory by getting your overdue invoice, or a managed inventory to allow one to have extra inventory that can be accessed when needed and at any time. This service not only frees up space and saves money, but also gives you the opportunity to focus on other things.

In addition, these services also offer free packaging checks to ensure that your packaging meets your requirements, helping you to reduce costs. They also help in stock control and improve efficiency, allowing one to move forward with their business.

In general, if you haven't thought about customizing your product, it's time to start thinking about it.

Do you have a blog or a website?

This section is a little more advanced... And it's for people who already have a blog or a website, but if you still don't have any of the above, this can serve you much later.

(do not worry if you do not understand much this section, in short, the purpose of this, is to bring your followers of instagram, your blog or website, to buy your products or hire your services)

Your site and blog is something you should be proud of. Most likely you have invested your money and time to make it a great tool to serve your customers and also to generate potential customers. However, is the inclusion of external links to your site the best idea? Links can keep people away from your site or distract them from reading your content.

Do not worry, links are a common practice expected and also respected by all types of users, so it is unlikely to damage your site. Here are four benefits you can get by including external links to your sites or blogs;

1. Makes your blog or website a more valuable and scalable resource

-

No matter how large your site may be, it can never contain all the relevant information or value a user may be looking for. Therefore, it makes a lot of sense to use the power of external links to create a scalable and easy path to make your website experience better and more rewarding visits. This not only rewards the brands you have linked to, but also gives your site the opportunity to become a reference resource.

2. Search engines are prone to reward behavior algorithmically -

Search engines spend time analyzing spam. In doing so, they look for links with quality signals rather than spam. While it's certainly worth considering the links you've used, the links you send can be useful and usable in the same way. Sites with low signal quality generally link to trash substantially compared to sites with high signal quality. These networks of trust and value can be used algorithmically by search engines to create better search results. Use this advantage and link to resources that you know your users, as well as the engines, will love.

4. *External links encourage positive contribution and participation*

There are many people on the web who are intelligent, talented and very dedicated who can contribute and make their efforts successful. When you include external links to your site, especially in a consistent and opportunity-oriented manner, you are creating incentives for website builders, forum participants and other users to commit to your site. Incentives bring value that will essentially build your site.

There are many good reasons why including external links is suitable for your site. To maximize your site, consider this as a tip.

Simple but powerful strategies to increase your followers

Having a great Instagram follow up can be very lucrative for marketing and driving free traffic to your site. But there's more than a simple set of numbers. The simple fact of having many followers does not necessarily mean anything. The key is to have active followers - people who not only follow you, but also like and comment on your messages. These are the people you want to address as you increase your audience.

We have all heard of people who buy Instagram followers, and although they have an impressive number of tens and hundreds of thousands, those followers mean nothing. They are purely aesthetic in nature. That's not what we're trying to do. We want to interact with our audience.

➤ *Be consistent*

There are some simple things we can implement to help our followers grow organically. The first is to publish consistently. This means that you want to publish once a day (or every other day, or twice a day, find what best suits your needs) and try to keep it more or less at the same time every day. But that's not all, it also means that you have to stick to a particular topic. Sure, you can absolutely post a beautiful landscape photo one day, and a photo from one computer game to the next, but the most beneficial thing is to keep a theme for all your messages.

➤ *Interact with your followers*

You've got the consistency down, and that's great, but it doesn't end there. You should also be interacting with the Instagram community. When someone comments on your message, take the time to recognize that comment, as if you like it, and respond to it. You will notice a greater interaction with time if you take the initiative to talk to your followers.

Their interaction doesn't stop at their posts. You should also spend time every day browsing the hashtags that are relevant to the information you share on Instagram. As you move around the site, it's important that you continue to enjoy and comment on the publications. What's the best way to attract people to your site? Show genuine appreciation for your site!

➤ *Gaining followers quickly by following and un-following*

If you are looking to quickly accumulate a large number of followers, there is a fairly simple and straightforward strategy you can follow that has proven its worth time and time again. This requires you to find pages with large followers that are similar in content to yours. Then, in addition to following the basic rules of publishing consistently within your topic, and maintaining constant interaction with your followers and the general community, you will go to the page of your choice and follow its followers. Typically, you want to continue between 25 and 35 in a single session. Then you should give them time to follow you back. If you want to increase your chances of getting a follower in return, you can like it and comment on some of their entries when you follow them. After you have given them time to follow you, you will unfold all of that page you have followed before. Then simply rinse and repeat, and you will find that the number of followers increases rapidly with real, quality followers.

The growth of your Instagram tracking can be very important for business purposes. If you follow the basic rules, publish high quality content and are willing to invest time and work, you can easily see an increase in followers almost immediately.

Attraction in Instagram

Statistics indicate that Instagram is one of the world's most popular social media sites, with at least 300 million active users per day. They contribute to more than 40 billion images shared on the platform to date. These figures have made Instagram the reference site for entrepreneurs looking to grow their business.

However, many people have used Instagram incorrectly, resulting in slow traction. Some of Instagram's leading personalities know that the secret to winning traction is organizing contests and draws to win attraction.

> ➢ *Contests*
> -

Contests are one of the proven ways to get the attraction, which gives you the opportunity to be openly creative with your content as possible. There are different types of contests you can organize, such as

Comment quizzes: - If the main objective is to generate feedback on your products or services and increase subsequent engagement, comment contests are the way forward. Simply upload a photo and ask your followers to comment on the post to have a chance to win the prize. Always ask your followers to tag other users.

Photo Contest: - Ask users to post a photo to their personal accounts and use a hashtag of their choice - this will help you find the tickets to choose a winner. To ensure attraction and desire, ask your followers and fans to creatively post photos of them using your product and/or service.

This type of contest can also include asking your fans to post one of your posts in order to have a chance to win.

> *Gifts*

The purpose of the competition is to attract the right fans, and the best way to find those users is to offer gifts that are relevant to your brand and your fans. The right types of gifts are those related to your brand, to bring the right type of interaction.

Simply give the rules in the subtitle section or provide a link to your website with a landing page that provides all the rules to get to win the draw. This allows you to keep your messages short and sweet.

It all comes down to spreading the word about your contests and sweepstakes. Hashtags are the best way to spread the word and keep track of entries. Look at the accounts of the leading companies in your niche and observe the type of hashtags they are using. The right combination of hashtags will increase the exposure of your contests and gifts, bringing more traction.

Conclusion: The video function of Instagram

Instagram's video content has become increasingly popular in social media recently, and is therefore extremely advantageous for anyone wishing to market themselves to make use of this feature. This change shows that more and more businesses, whether small or large, are beginning to communicate visually with their followers, customers and fans.

The video feature is one of the most popular platforms that will allow you to harness the power of marketing!

With more than 150 million users, Instagram is the best platform to share. It allows you to share not only photos but also short videos. There are millions and millions of videos shared daily, which is a great reason why one should use this platform. Below are some of the main advantages of using this function:

> ➤ *Greater commitment*

Unlike video entries on Twitter or Facebook, which are sometimes overlooked by users regardless of their quality, Instagram videos are rarely lost. According to a study by Forrester, Instagram videos generate more engagement 58 times than Facebook and 120 times than Twitter. Having an Instagram account with interesting and useful content can earn you one with crazy levels of engagement with the audience.

➢ **Building Personality and Trust**

As content is becoming increasingly popular, one of the main advantages of using the video feature is that it helps build trust. People buy from people they can trust, and the Instagram video feature will help you create that emotional connection with your audience. The most important thing here is that this feature allows you to share your daily experience in an informal and informal way, giving fans, fans and customers a sense of business.

Sharing activities behind the scenes has been identified as a good example for Instagram, especially if it is a service provider. These videos make the company more reliable and attractive, which in turn has a positive impact on the marketing of the company.

➢ **Increased traffic**

Although you can't add links to videos, they're still a dominant source of traffic. In addition, with engagement levels higher than Twitter and Facebook, the use of the video feature can be tremendously useful for your site's visibility.

➢ **Gaining a competitive advantage**

Competition on Instagram is still much lower than on Twitter or Facebook. The American Express Survey reported that nearly 2% of small businesses are currently adopting the Instagram video feature and have gained an advantage over their competitors. Therefore, it is clear that by using the video feature, you are likely to reach your target audience faster and easier.

➢ *Free advertising*

Yeah, that's right. The great thing about using the Instagram video function is free advertising. One can show your services and products in action generating a great exposure. The feature gives you the opportunity to show what you are offering.

Accept the video feature and you'll be rewarded!

Now yes, I wish you the best in your results, and remember, everything is practical; theory without action is of no use to you.

A big hug, your friend, Gaston!

By the way, when you achieve your results little by little, I highly recommend you, if you want to learn much more about methods of earning money, my book, on "MAKING MONEY WITH YOUR PINTEREST ACCOUNT", is a book that I'm sure will help you a lot on your way to "financial freedom". Without further ado, you can find it in the Amazon search engine, like: "Make money with your pinterest account" or looking for my name, like: "Gaston Echevarria"... Once again I wish you success in your results!

www.ingramcontent.com/pod-product-compliance
Lightning Source LLC
Chambersburg PA
CBHW072033230526
45468CB00021B/1660